T0171661

MUSTARD SEED MIRACLES

Keith Mugglestone

authorHOUSE®

AuthorHouse™ UK
1663 Liberty Drive
Bloomington, IN 47403 USA
www.authorhouse.co.uk
Phone: 0800.197.4150

Published by AuthorHouse 01/27/2015

ISBN: 978-1-5049-3663-7 (sc)
ISBN: 978-1-5049-3662-0 (hc)
ISBN: 978-1-5049-3664-4 (e)

Chapter 1

"In The Beginning Was The Word." John 1;1

My story begins in the late 1930's and my bedroom was the small room at the front of the house that overlooked the main road. Every Sunday morning I was awoken by a man who used to push his bicycle down the road and stop every 200-300 yards and he would open his bible and begin to proclaim the word of God. What he proclaimed did not register with me at the age of 7, but the example of his persistence and determination to do this come Hail, Rain or Shine remained with me as a memory for the rest of my life.

As a child I went to a local Sunday school and heard the stories about Jesus and prayer. During the week I attended a private school about 2 miles away from my home we often walked to school and would take a short cut through the town. We used to pass a small house with a yard surrounded by a brick wall. The lady of the house had a small dog, a black and white rough haired terrier, which had just delivered 6 puppies. We could see the puppies out in the yard.

Every day I would look at these puppies and there was one with a black patch over one eye and one ear and I knew that this was to be my dog. I told Mum and Dad about this and we had the usual conversation," dogs are a great responsibility and that I was not yet old enough to care for one". Eventually, by persistence, I wore them down and brought Patch home with me. Every day as I came home from school he would run down the path to the front gate to greet me. We had great games romping and playing together in the garden.

One day I came home from school and Patch did not come to me, so I asked Mum" Have you seen Patch" and she answered "No. didn't he come to meet you" So we began to search for this lost dog, we searched the house and the garden and couldn't find him anywhere. When Dad came home from work we told him about this problem and he reminded me that" I did warn you that if that little dog ever got onto this busy main road that would be the end of him". However Dad went through the village telling all the neighbours and everyone else that the little dog was missing.

Eventually it came round to bedtime and I went to bed and tried to sleep, it was summer time and with the long days the sunlight came in through the curtains. I found that I couldn't get off to sleep and I lay there thinking about my lost dog and remembering things about Sunday school and praying and about how Jesus loves little children. So I thought that I would pray and see what Jesus could do about it. At that time I had no idea how to pray "properly" so I just talked to God/Jesus about my problem.

Later on Mum came up and said "now Keith you must settle down, there is School in the morning" after she had gone back downstairs I began to pray again. Eventually I tired and went to sleep.

The next day I came home from school and there was still no dog and no news about him and again that night bedtime became Prayer Time. I prayed and Mum came to tell me to settle down and eventually, I tired and went to sleep. On the third day (and that might be significant!!) I began to pray again at bedtime and I was getting desperate by now as this was becoming serious as far as I was concerned. I was talking to Jesus along the lines that "this dog should not be lost, cold and starving. So that if you cannot return him to me then at least make sure he has a good home that will care for him. OF COURSE If you could send him back to me that would be much better and if you could manage this, then in the future I will go anywhere and do whatever you ask of me."

AT THAT MOMENT there was a knock at the back door of the house and as Dad went to see who was there I heard a big gruff Derbyshire miner's voice say "Aye up Fred is this thee Pup?" it was and I went to sleep that night a Very Happy Bunny.

My childhood continued and I went to Sunday school and joined the church choir. Later on I became a Sunday school teacher and began to play the church organ. In due course I took school exams, went to college and completed my training as a Pharmacist. Then the time for National Service arrived. (Which had to be endured.) My leisure activities at that time were; Tennis and Badminton and GIRLS, Ballroom dancing and GIRLS and then Motorbikes and GIRLS.

As release from National Service approached I felt ready to begin "My Life" which comprised marriage, a family and a business. I needed to find the right girl, there had been a painful failed relationship during National Service and I was still having difficulty with this. Mum was aware of this and she confided in a friend who sang with her in a nearby local choir. Her friend responded by saying that," I know of a young lady who is a school teacher in a very similar situation. So we exchanged addresses, corresponded and eventually met. Things progressed rapidly as we both realised that this was IT. We arranged to get married in January.

I was still completing National Service and was due to be released in September. I used to phone Jean every Thursday for a chat, and one Thursday she announced that she wanted to postpone the wedding which threw me right off balance.

I borrowed a sergeant's car and dashed off for 120 miles to see Jean. Because THIS WAS MY GIRL and I was not going to let her get lost or disappear for any reason whatsoever. She agreed (very kindly) to give up her idea of a Spring -Wedding and we would stick to the original date.

We were married in January and flew to Paris for our honeymoon. In those days that was quite an adventure. We had a wonderful time and even hired a motor scooter to ride around Paris. One morning we were driving down the Champs Elysee which at that time had about 5 lanes in both directions. When the traffic lights changed every one just took off with all the power they had. We set off on the scooter and Jean was wearing her pretty going away hat which blew off into the road, immediately all of the Paris traffic stopped and several young men leaped out of their cars to rescue Madam' s Chapeau. Perhaps it may still happen in Paris I don't Know?

Shortly after we returned we bought a small pharmacy and a house in a small township near to Jean's Parents.

Chapter 2

The Storm Clouds begin to Gather

For the first two or three years the business developed and after the first years trading my accountants wrote to congratulate us on the increase in turnover from the previous owners results, they said that if we could maintain this then we would have a viable business.

Over the next couple of years we noticed that some of the terraced cottages were being demolished and the people were being re-housed elsewhere. This produced a small reduction in turnover but we hoped to compensate for this. However this demolition process continued and we began to find ourselves isolated in a bleak building site.

Our first child was expected and Jean would soon need to stop teaching, there was no way that the Pharmacy alone with its reduced turnover would provide a living for a family. So we had to take some hard decisions and be prepared to write off the loss that we would have to face when this business finally died.

Even during this time Jean and I still felt that God must know what He is doing so we decided "to bite the bullet" and move on.

I was offered a job by one of our creditors to help us in this situation. This job provided a good wage and living accommodation. So our immediate needs were provided for, and we accepted his offer gratefully.

Our daughter Wendy was born at this time and we wanted to resolve our remaining business problems as soon as we were able. I decided to offer my services as a locum Pharmacist, taking over for other pharmacists for holidays, ill health and so on. This would mean much travelling and being away from home for most of the week but the income was much greater and we were determined that every one of our debts would be paid off in full as soon as possible.

We decided to move to the Home Counties and we hoped to take advantage of the way property values in the South were increasing. We managed to scrape together enough for a deposit on a small house I then placed an advert in the professional journal offering myself as a Locum.

I was approached by a brewery firm who were planning to open off-licences combined with a pharmacy on new housing estates. They would need a qualified pharmacist at each premise and my position was to provide relief as and when necessary. Eventually the business expanded to the extent that I became a sort of trouble shooter/problem solver over the whole chain from Scotland to the South Coast.

I came across an interesting situation in one of the Pharmacies. The manager was newly qualified and began to suffer from depression. This developed to the extent that one night the Police found him sleep walking in his pyjamas down a fast dual carriage way. They took care of the immediate problem, but of course next morning my phone rang and could I get down there and sort something out. When I arrived the poor chap was completely out of balance and all he wanted to do was to tell me about the number of cracks he could see in the ceiling.

He was admitted to hospital and one of the conditions of this type of employment is that the accommodation is tied to the job. So it was necessary for his furniture to be placed in storage and a temporary arrangement made for his wife and family whilst he was receiving treatment.

I travelled daily for the next few weeks until another Pharmacist manager could be appointed. Our second child was due very soon and I was not too happy about being away at this particular time. One day, after lunch, I had a feeling that, "you need to be at home" it was nothing dramatic just a feeling. You need to be at home. So I put a notice on the door, closed the Pharmacy and left the staff to carry on with the day to day business. Then I drove 70 miles back home

When I arrived at about 4 o-clock Jean was in very advanced labour. She had called the midwife earlier who decided "it is not happening yet" and she would call in again in the evening to see how things were progressing. But, Neal was not going to wait for the evening. So I had to assist as best I could. Just as he was born the door bell rang and the midwife had called back. She arrived just in time to finish off.

Jean and I are both convinced that God had His hand on this situation.

It is surprising how some people see miracles and others don't.

Obviously if you don't believe then you won't see.

Chapter 3

The Climb Back

For the next two years we lived in the South of England and continued with Locum work for the same Company. By keeping our expenses to a minimum we were able to begin to pay off all our debts. We were surprised how, even in this situation, when we made contact with our creditors and promised to honour our commitments they were all prepared to trust us and be patient.

During that time property values more than doubled, and this gave us the opportunity to move back to our native Derbyshire and purchase an architect designed house in its own grounds, for less than we sold the house in the South of England for.

Truly God is sovereign in every situation and over every difficulty.

The locum work still provided an excellent backup and since I have always been interested in things mechanical and electrical I had designed a few tools and car accessories and we began to market these by Mail Order. The business expanded and over the years we saw the growth of a successful business.

We now had all the worldly things. A house in its own grounds with a swimming pool, we were members of the Rotary Club and I owned an Aston Martin.

But we both knew that there needed to be more than this.!!

However we were now so involved with the business and "The World" with its values, that in order to make the change to a more Spiritual life style we would have to relocate again.

We decided to look towards rural Lincolnshire for a small farm property with outbuildings in the yard which would serve for workshop space, and we had the usual list of requirements for our ideal property. This included about 2 acres of land for the children and their donkey, I would like some water frontage where I could moor my boat and we wanted to be no more than 15minutes down a decent road to a useful town.

So we moved our boat to a mooring on the river and began to visit every weekend and search the estate agents lists. We did this for three years and found that it was not going to be as easy as we had imagined. When we found a property that suited our list, we could not afford it, and when we did find one that we could afford, it did not fit the list.

At this time we began to realise that the dream was becoming more and more distant as property values were rising and the stock of suitable ones was diminishing.

We could not quite understand this as we felt very strongly that we were following God's leading.

We decided that we should give up on this dream for the time being, at least, and return to Derbyshire. We set off in the boat to go back home, on the river there is a visitors mooring in a small village. We had often stopped here for a visit and we decided to moor up here for one last time before we left for good. As we walked across the road, I saw an estate agent setting up a For Sale sign at the entrance to a drive down the side of a small waterway. I walked down to have a look, it was a small farm house with a yard and out buildings as well. It was absolutely ideal and I agreed to purchase it, at the asking price, there and then. Even though we had not yet put our property on the market.

On our return to Derbyshire I needed to sell our home and placed an advert in the next issue of the local paper. Within 48 hours we had agreed a sale for the full asking price, to a first time buyer, with no property chain to worry about.

When God moves it is wonderful to see how He moves

We made the move to Lincolnshire in due course and the next stage of our life began.

Still Water cottage

Chapter 4

Grow well little Seed

We arrived in Lincolnshire in 1977, the year of the Queen's Silver Jubilee. The village organised a celebration evening, we were invited to attend and this gave us the opportunity to meet and greet the whole local community. The local vicar was present and came to have a word with us, later that week he called at our home and invited us to attend the local church.

We were pleased to do this and felt that we ought to serve the church and local community, we began to attend regularly and gradually we were asked to become more involved in church affairs. The church had recently been given an electric organ to replace the old one which was pumped by working two pedals. The organist was a dear lady who had to wear a calliper on one leg and she was afraid of this new organ in case the electricity went up the calliper and into her leg. After having struggled for some time with this difficulty she felt that she could not manage this "new thing". So I was asked to play the organ.

The vicar had suffered from diabetes for many years and this disease often attacks the eyesight after a long period, and his was beginning to fail. At one service he was delivering his sermon and everyone noticed that he started to turn away from us until eventually he was preaching to the wall with his back to us. As usual in these situations no one seems willing to take the initiative and do something. So I got out of my seat, went up to him and quietly explained what had happened, I turned him in the right direction and stayed with him until he finished the service.

Over the next few weeks he encouraged me to begin to train as a lay reader and my relationship with God began to deepen and I found that the more I realised the magnitude of His love, the deeper my love for Him grew. I soon began to understand that the only possible response to God's love is a complete commitment to serve Him ONLY according to His will and in accordance to His Word.

At this time I began to realise that something serious was about to happen, so I told my family; my wife Jean, daughter Wendy and son Neal that I felt called to become a full time committed Christian and that whilst I could do this on my own, it would be better if we could agree to do this as a family. I was delighted when they all responded immediately and agreed.

As our understanding grew, we had to learn to live along the lines that our purpose was to follow Gods purpose as it is in the book.

If it's in the Book. Do It;

If the Book says don't do it …….. Don't.

Our Battle cry became as Joshua 24:15. "As for me and my household we will serve the Lord."

God was preparing us for His purpose. What that purpose was we didn't yet know or understand, but of course we didn't need to because His plans are always for our good and not to harm us. Jer. 29:11.

As my call became clearer my message to the local churches became sharper, and the vicar said to me one day "your trouble is that you are too radical ". The congregations resented this and eventually this door was closed, and I was led to Rev3:7 "These are the words of Him who is holy and true, what he opens no one can shut and what he shuts no one can open. See, I have placed before you an open door that no one can shut, I know that you have little strength, yet you have kept my word and have not denied my name".

I felt that I had been put through this in order that I may be made,

FIT FOR PURPOSE. Whatever that would turn out to be.

So once again we were solely reliant on God and had been cast out into the wilderness.

My business continued to demand regular daily attention and I would walk around the yard considering all these things ………and a song, by Chris Bowater, took hold of my mind and would not let me go.

I sang it all day and for many days.

Do something new, Lord
In my heart, make a start
Do something new, Lord
Do something new

I open up my heart
As much as can be known
I open up my will
To conform to yours alone

I lay before your feet
All my hopes and my desires
Unreservedly submit
To what Your Spirit may require

I only want to live
For Your pleasure now
I long to please You, Father
Will you show me how?

It would be only a short while before God revealed His answer to that request, in the meantime we continued with the day to day routine.

At this time we were manufacturing a range of shower cubicles of our own design which required no permanent connections to main services. This made them a tenant's fixture and they could be moved from place to place. There was a small market for this design in England but we found a bigger one in Sweden for their leisure homes were often situated in the mountain regions.

In the winter the temperature is sub zero and it is not practical to provide a mains water supply so our design filled this bill perfectly.

I employed the services of a Swedish marketing firm to develop this opportunity and it was arranged that one of the large Swedish manufacturers of bathroom equipment would produce and market our design under licence.

I visited Sweden again for a meeting with the board of this Company and we agreed terms, this was a very exciting breakthrough for us. I had the draft contract in my briefcase and was preparing to return to England to have the details checked and approved and we were to be in business in a much greater way.

I was staying in the home of our agent and I needed to set off in the small hours of the morning to drive to the ferry the next day. So I went to bed early for a good nights sleep. However I was so excited by our success that I could not sleep. So I spent some time on my knees thanking God and praising Him for this wonderful blessing. I was so thrilled and grateful that I soon ran out of sufficient words to express this, and I found that I was speaking in a different way entirely. The Holy Spirit had given me my own special language so that I would always be able to communicate with Him even when I did not always understand every detail.

I was also shown during this prayer time that I must not allow this new opportunity to overshadow everything else. I was reminded that I had chosen to be His servant and the business was to be a means to that end.

Chapter 5

Do Something New Lord

When I returned to England, the new business routine settled down, Our son Neal completed his schooling and decided to join the business. Our daughter Wendy was away at Durham University reading for her degree in theology.

Our plan was that Neal would gradually take over an increasing responsibility in the business and I would be able to devote more time to God's Work.

After the lessons of the last few months I was even more convinced that my calling was to spread The Word and reach out to as many as The Lord would put before me. This became a belief which was to remain with me until the present time..

I was to be, merely, just a sower. The nurturing and harvesting would be The Lord's business.

Wendy completed her degree and returned home to assist us in the office and for a few months we were able to work with a small ministry which equipped Mini Vans as mobile Christian Libraries to loan out the books to people who would invite them to visit.

Neal and Wendy took over one of these vans and visited people with the books. As they went around in the local villages they found that The Word was rarely proclaimed because many of the churches and chapels had closed due to depopulation.

Which re-ignited my desire to spread "The Word" in such places.

We bought a large single deck bus, and fitted it out as a mobile library with books and audio tapes in the entrance. The main body was used as a meeting room with a counselling and prayer area at the rear.

Bus Photo

When "The Bus" was ready, we were all nervous as to the reception we might receive and as we were about to set of on its first venture there was a very heavy rain storm. So our departure was delayed. Then as the storm lifted we saw a brilliant full Rainbow which spanned "The Bus" from stem to stern. We saw this as a definite confirmation so we set off. We tried to visit at least one or two villages a week and soon had a busy schedule. I would drive the bus to the parking site, Wendy would follow in the car and she would meet the young Mum's and the little ones as they came out from school in the afternoon. I would return to work and then in the evening we would all go to the bus for an evening meeting.

In one small town there was a group of lively young men who used to congregate in the market square where we parked and they thought it would be great fun to cause a disturbance.

I went out to talk to them and suggested that if they would let us "old folk" have our meeting then, afterwards, Neal would take them to the local "chippy" and they could come back with their chips onto The Bus and we could discuss anything they liked. And believe me they discussed far and wide.

Bus interior

The local Police came to see us when we visited again a few weeks later and they told us that since our visits began the town was much quieter in the evening.

In another place the local Elim church asked us to attend and lead one of their evening meetings, and there we met Ginger Powers an American lady who was spending some time with them to help redecorate their church.

She had spent her life as an evangelist, mainly in Marseille France, in the dockland area witnessing to the seamen who came in on the ships. She told many stories of God's provision, protection, and care.

One evening in our home village, we were rehearsing together on The Bus for a carol service that we were to perform over the Christmas period. One of our village neighbours walked down to see us and said that he had heard "heavenly music from his garden" and he had come to see what it was. He also said to me "there is something different about your family, do you take vitamins or supplements?" It gave me the opportunity to explain things to him.

Another small fellowship invited us to join with them for an evening meeting. They met in a small disused wooden building and when we entered the service was just beginning.

At the front of the hall there was a young lady playing the piano and both Jean and I noticed our son Neal's reaction when he saw this young lady. Her name was Davina and in due course she became Neal's wife. She joined the family firm and also the ministry team.

It is so delightful how God provides for all His children's needs.

During this time we began to realise this more and more strongly. Our business continued steadily and we have never had to ask for financial help for Gods work. He always provided exactly what was needed but only when it was needed.

Customers used to visit us, and they would see The Bus parked in the yard and they also saw our small business. They often commented "how do you manage to do all this with just this".

Then once again we entered into one of England's seemingly regular recessions, sales and earnings were down and winter was coming on.

One Monday morning, I was in the office talking to The Lord about this difficulty when the phone rang.

I answered and a young man asked "are you Bermuda Showers?" He proceeded to tell me that He and a friend had been very disappointed by his church's Harvest Festival service a few weeks ago. So they decided to offer their own thanks to God by providing an evening meal for The Birmingham City Mission. (providing shelter for homeless men.)

After the meal, they were talking to the superintendent and they asked "what is your greatest need." He told them, The Mission desperately needed 2 shower units as they had minimal washing facilities for the men.

It now became obvious who had caused them to phone us!

I was very aware of our own difficulties but was beginning to realise that "faith is the substance of things not yet seen" so I said that I would be happy to donate two complete shower units, however I could not spend the time away from work to install them in Birmingham, if they could find an electrician and a plumber in their church who would volunteer do the installation then I would donate and deliver the showers to The Mission. The installation was completed successfully.

It was to be several years later before I would be allowed to see God's purpose in this.

Of course we still had to deal with our difficulties and I calculated that we needed to earn at least £3000 to take us through the winter when hopefully things would improve. I continued to talk to The Lord about this along these lines.

The "ideal" solution that I had in mind involved a Rolls Royce coming down the drive with a man who would offer me a contract that would be worth £3000 ("your thoughts are not my thoughts says The Lord"!!)

I was spending a few moments looking up the drive to the main road and it was raining with that fine penetrating mist that soaks though to the skin.

Then I saw a man on a bicycle coming towards us (Definitely not a Rolls Royce)

He came round to the office door and knocked. When I answered he said "I've come to see if you can offer me any work." My first thought was, that is exactly what I need my friend.

However I said "come on in, take off your wet coat, have a cup of tea and tell me all about it".

He told me that he had travelled 30 miles to see us because a firm that he knew had advised him to contact us, since we were going to build a machine for them, and that he should ask if we would give him the electrical installation work when the time came.

I said that I had no knowledge of this at all but that if he would give me the firms phone no. I would follow this up immediately, and that he could most certainly have the installation work if this came to fruition and would he give me his own name and address so that there could be no slip up later on. He told me that this was not necessary as the firm knew him well.

He then took his leave and mounted his bicycle. I looked through the office window a few seconds later to watch as he departed and there was no sign of him

I phoned the number that he had given. They were a private company and yes they did need such a machine. I went over that afternoon and the deal was made

When the time came for the electrical work to be done I enquired about the man that had come to see me. The director told me that he had no idea what I was talking about as he knew of no such man.

The net profit on that work was EXACTLY £3000

Did I entertain an Angel unaware? - I know I did.

Chapter 6

A Time to Consolidate

The Bus ministry was now functioning well and business was good.

The bible tells us "that to all things there is a time and a season. We had been busy planting seeds from both The Bus and the business, but we did not always see an immediate response.

We understood this to some extent but our faith was to be tested and strengthened some more.

We continued with the bus visits and began to build relationships with many of the churches that we visited. In some places we received encouragement and at other times resistance or rejection.

We found that in the "good" times it was not difficult to be faithful.

However during the "bad" times being faithful required much more determination, and so we continued to do the work that God had put before us.

There were some very good times,

In one AOG church the pastor also had a heart for evangelism and encouraged us enormously. We were able to attend their services together as a family for several years, although we could only be visitors because of our own work.

And again

Many years previously when our children were still at school, one of Neal's school friends was a member of a tiny Methodist church which stood alone in farm land miles from any village. They had just been given permission for a mains electricity supply and the two lads must have discussed this at school. The family that supported this small church were trying to install the system at minimum cost and I think that Neal might have said "my Dad could do that". It was soon agreed that they would provide the materials and that I and one of our lads would install it.

This led to a relationship with that lovely body of Christians for many years to come.

There were occasional bad times as well.

Some times when we arrived for a visit to a place we found that the parking site that we used had been deliberately blocked.

And again,

We visited one village hall where we parked, and the superintendent said that we would be welcome anytime. On the next visit we were told that the committee had decided that we should not come again.

Through all of this The Lord continued to support and encouraged us in every imaginable way. Finances, Health, Family relationships and a "Peace and Joy that is past understanding".

We continued to learn that, "sowers' sow, and God is the gardener and He will produce His planned results in His time

This released us from any need to look for justification from results.

That is God's problem.

All we had to do was to

Keep on sowing, When ever, Where ever, and However.

as God gave us the opportunity

As a result of all this we were being taught Endurance. God encouraged us in this time by allowing us to see signs of growth in some people sometimes.

There was a young boy 6 years old who used to come on the bus when we visited his village. He would arrive after school and just sit down and look and listen.

He would stay and share our sandwiches with us and then he stayed for the first evening meeting. At about 7 o-clock he would say "I have to go home now."

This happened on every visit to that village for about two and a half years. We do not know what happened, but God will not waste that opportunity.

There was another young lady (late twenties?) who used to come regularly, she was very reserved and shy but she did reveal that she lived some miles away from the town in a very remote hamlet. It was winter time and the nights were dark early, so we suggested that Jean and I would give her a lift home after the meeting. She directed us to her house and said "please don't come in Father will be very cross."

She visited the Bus regularly through the winter but we never got to meet her father.

One Sunday afternoon some months later, I was taking an afternoon service in a church some miles away from this young lady's home. The service had begun, when the church door opened and a very wet person arrived dressed in Motorcycle waterproof clothing. Everyone looked round and as usual no-one seemed to know what to do. So I walked down the aisle to find her a seat, hymn book etc and then we resumed.

After the service I went to talk to her and she was the person who used to visit The Bus. She had travelled on her Moped many miles to this church in very bad weather "just to be in fellowship with Christians she knew."

That spring, as Easter time came near we felt that as a family we needed time with God and His people somewhere away from our usual venues. We made contact with a Christian guest house at a coastal resort and asked if we could all travel up in our ministry Bus to stay with them over Easter.

They made us all very welcome. The young men (Neal and Wendy's boyfriend, Philip) slept on The Bus and the girls in the guest house. It was run by a couple who had been in The Lords service for most of their lives and they also led worship services in a small chapel which we were able to attend.

That weekend break provided us with so much more than the respite we needed..

It provided an opening for many years of shared ministry in that church and friendship with that lovely couple.

You see. Once again God opens doors that we do not even imagine could be there.

We serve an awesome God

Chapter 7

Once Again The Scene Changes

Our two young people were growing and maturing and we could see clearly that in the next few years there would be some important changes.

We knew by now, that we did not need to see the details of those changes. We were content to move by faith and expect to be delighted.

Everybody had settled into God's service with The Bus and also the AOG church where we worshiped on Sunday.

Our daughter was the first to move when, she married Philip and I was privileged to conduct their Wedding.

They set up home in a village abut 12 miles away from the family and joined a Spirit Filled church in their nearest town. They both began to serve in that church and soon entered into leadership.

About a year later Neal and Davina were married and again I was able to perform the ceremony for them.

Neal and Davina took over the family home and they joined the business as full partners. Neal began to take over an increasing management role and they both continued in service with the AOG church.

This released Jean and I for whatever God might have in store for us. Since we wanted to be available for" Whatever Whenever However" we set up a temporary mobile home in the Orchard of the house and bought a large old Motor Cruiser. We began to use this to cruise the Inland waterways and gradually increased the times that we were away, to give Neal and Davina the opportunity to take over the day to day management more and more.

About this time we received an offer from an old business associate to buy The Bus. They were Catholics and intended to use it for evangelism within their Diocese. They wanted it converted for living accommodation as well, we were able to do this for them and when the work was completed they set off to serve God in whatever way He would call them.

There was still a small demand for us to visit one or two of "our" villages so we set up another smaller bus for these faithful village fellowships. This worked for a time but we could see that after 6 years we had done as much as could be done. There were two reasons for this.

People had become accustomed to The Bus and it was no longer a new thing.

Secondly there was a limit to the radius we could cover from our base for a daily visit. This was about 30 miles mainly because buses are not high speed vehicles on local country roads.

We could feel that something new was being provided, and all we had to do was wait for it

Around this time our business expanded rapidly, almost overnight, We had been hoping for a wider market for our Shower unit and the danger of asbestos insulation in buildings was suddenly acknowledged by the authorities.

This started a rush to remove this materiel safely and quickly. One of the requirements for removal was that it must be done in a sealed environment and that the operatives must change their clothes on entry and exit from the site, by passing through an air lock which included a decontamination shower facility.

We needed only a few days to convert our unit from its pretty domestic appearance to a more robust unit suitable for industrial use.

It took several years for this asbestos material to be removed from most of the affected buildings and our unit became one of the main pieces of equipment in use. We supplied individual contractors as well as government projects and the military. We even sent a batch out to a desert in the Middle East for use on oil rig exploration sites.

We began to see that this really did set us free for "Whatever Whenever Wherever"

During this time our five grandchildren started to arrive and we were still using the boat along with our mobile home and serving with local churches most weekends.

One Sunday afternoon a couple walked down to call upon us and told us they were on a boat moored at the lock in our village and had enquired about a local church and had been sent to see us.

We spent a time of fellowship and prayer with them and discovered that they were moving their narrow boat, called King David, by road to France where they hoped to cruise the French waterways during their retirement.

They set sail the following day but it had been a pleasant meeting with two very interesting people. We were to discover them and King David again much later in France.

All our boats have been called "Amazing Grace" for obvious reasons. We realised that the time had come to replace the first "Amazing Grace". I had always wanted to build a complete boat from the ground upwards and felt that this would be my chance. So I commissioned a marine architect to design a 15M boat with comfortable accommodation for a couple and strong enough for both river and sea work. We were content to see how God would use this and we were leaving the situation entirely open to Him.

Amazing Grace

On one trip on the river Trent we passed a private mooring where a boat called "Born Again" was moored. So we just had to turn round and moor alongside to investigate. The owner of the property came out because, no doubt, he had often encountered people trying to use his mooring. When he read the name of our boat "Amazing Grace", his attitude changed and we spent a good afternoon with he and his wife.

He had spent a life time as an evangelist and had started his work in the Market place of Jeans' home town. He now led a local fellowship which had expanded over the years, planting churches in various places in England.

It is wonderful how God puts His people together for their delight.

AND ONCE AGAIN GOD MOVED.

I was in the office one Saturday morning just clearing up a few odds and ends from the week and I had a look at the post just in case there was anything urgent.

One of the letters carried foreign stamps and was from India. Now I knew no-one in India, had never been to India and did not particularly wish to visit India.

However I had learned that God moves in some very interesting ways so I opened the letter and read it.

It was from a Pastor of a church and Children's home located in an area which had just experienced their worst flood for 40 years and they were in great difficulty. He told me that God had prompted him to write this letter to me.

I did not feel able to dismiss this lightly especially since the envelope was addressed absolutely correctly, to me at the Company even down to the Postcode.

So I replied immediately saying that I regarded his letter very seriously and that I would come out on the first available flight.

And now The New Scene opens

Chapter 8

A New Scene opens

As we approached this new work, the whole family realised that this would be our greatest step out into the unknown so far.

In the past we had all tried to follow Heb10:38 "my righteous one will live by faith. And if he shrinks back I will not be pleased with him". The result of our previous mistakes was that we learned that Faith comes by perseverance.

Every time we miss our target, we get up, dust ourselves down and start again. Each time our determination is toughened.

Having posted my reply to India the next step was to visit local Reference library and gain some information. The first thing I learned was that there were two towns in India with the same name as the one I was planning to visit. One was in the extreme North and one in the South. I was unable to deduce from the Indian letter which would be the right one to choose. So once again from the very first tentative step everything was to be in God's hands and I was only the errand boy.

Bombay seemed to be a point of entry roughly equidistant between the two possible destinations so I went onto the internet and paid for an economy flight to Bombay departing in two weeks time. Shortly afterwards I found out that I needed a visa to visit India. Since time was short Jean and I went to the Indian high commission to apply for a visa in person.

We found ourselves in an enormous waiting room with many people waiting for service. There was a ticket system in operation we took our ticket which was number 239 and the current number on display about No 60. So we thought we could be in for a long wait. Eventually I was called to the desk and submitted my application form and then went back to wait some more.

I was soon called again and was told that I must see the Deputy High Commissioner. When I entered his office he said that the form was incorrect. In the space where I had to declare the purpose of my visit I stated that I was visiting the pastor and his people in response to his letter.

The Commissioner regarded this as Christian Missionary work and I must fill in another form which would take more than 18 months to process. I explained that this was God's work and I had already purchased my ticket and would be leaving within 48 hours.

It soon became obvious that I had a problem, so I stated that as God's servant I may not argue with him, but that my wife and I would return to the waiting room and begin to pray for God to intervene.

About 10 or 15 minutes later, the man appeared with a new form and pointed to, "the purpose of visit" box, and he said "Put in tourist" he then gave me my passport complete with a visa stamp. Hallelujah and PTL.

In due course my plane landed at Bombay and I made my first contact with India. The tourist brochures describe India as a land of mystery and beauty, as I rode in the taxi towards the centre of Bombay I saw that there was very little mystery about the poverty I saw everywhere. How can squalor, filth, hunger and disease be described as beauty? I suppose that this is the "third world culture shock" that people experience on their first visit. I felt that I must never allow myself to become accustomed to this. Here was real need although I had no clue as to how I could possibly have an effect on such a massive and seemingly insurmountable problem. However I believed, that once again, God knew what He was doing and that He would provide whatever and wherever as usual.

I needed to find a hotel and then make enquiries at the railway station for my journey to the right destination bearing in mind that there were two towns with the same name. I asked the taxi driver to take me to a hotel and then to wait so that he could take me to the Station. The hotel was suitable and at the station I showed the ticket clerk my letter from the pastor with his address on the letterhead. I was given a ticket and was told that I would have to change at Hyderabad. So far so good!

The train left in the evening of the following day so I had time to explore and discover real Indian food. I have always had an interest in boats and ships so I wandered toward the dock area hoping to see some activity. I was soon approached by a young man who asked me," would you like a good clean girl sir" This was not the sort of activity I had hoped for so I did an immediate about turn and got out of there as fast as possible..

The journey was uneventful, the train travelled overnight to arrive at Hyderabad the next morning. The connection did not leave until the evening and I found that the station had rest rooms which could be rented quite cheaply. I did not want to leave the station complex and miss the train, so I stayed in the room and had meals in the restaurant until it was time to leave

I found the correct platform and there was my train. Each coach has a list pasted on the side with the names and seat numbers of everyone who has booked to travel. I checked every coach and my name was nowhere to be found. All the coaches were full and departure time was getting close. I spotted a first class compartment with a vacant seat, I was not going to miss this train,

So I got on and sat down. I would explain the situation and offer to pay the extra charge for the first class travel.

The ticket collector came and made it very clear that this was NOT in accordance with regulations, I did not yet have any Indian money and he refused to accept English. One of the passengers offered to change a £5 note for rupees and after some more discussion the collector accepted the payment. Bedtime came and we folded down the seats to make beds and tried to go to sleep.

Eventually morning came and the train came to a stop at a station. The stations all have a name board in both Hindu script and English. (Thank you Lord). This station did not have the name of my destination, and I was determined that I would only get off at the right place. Eventually I was left alone in the compartment and a porter came to say "you must get off here"

The flood damage had washed away the train track and the train could go no further

Damaged Rail Track

So I found myself in a strange town with no idea how far it was to my destination or how to get there. When you've reached the limit of your own abilities then God will always provide for those who trust, obey and believe.

There was a group of taxi drivers talking in the station yard so I approached them to explain my predicament. Many Indians have some English which made it possible for us understand each other.

They said they could reach the address on my, by now, well worn Indian letter. Each one was willing to take me and they began to bid against each other to offer the lowest price. I had to make a decision so I had a look at their tyres and chose the one with the most tread remaining.

We set off and I could soon see the damage, the rail track hung in space across a washed out river bed, and as we went through the villages many of the houses were reduced to rubble and the taxi sometimes had to negotiate around these obstacle., Eventually we came to a stop because the road was completely blocked by fallen houses.

A group of children came out to see who had come and they gathered around and chattered. Eventually the taxi driver managed to quieten them and he said with a big grin. You have arrived" this is your place."

I got down from the taxi, paid and thanked the driver, the children took charge of my bag and led me, only a few yards to the "Faith Orphan's Home" and I met the pastor.

Chapter 9

I Meet Christians In India

After I had arrived and settled in at the home of the Pastor, I found that when Indians become Christian they change their name from their Hindu one to a new Christian name. I will call this pastor. James.

The next morning I was taken on a walk around the village to see results of the flood. There was almost total devastation, many of the homes had woven walls and roofs were made of banana leaf branches. These had just disappeared in the flood together with all the household contents. The better houses had mud brick walls and a thatched roof but again flood water softens and dissolves mud brick.

I understood that in the monsoon season this was a natural event and they usually made repairs and carried on, but the magnitude of this flood had taken out the whole village at a stroke and there was no outside help forthcoming. The Authorities had been to see and promised help, but some weeks later nothing was happening.

A person from the village came to see me and asked "have you come from the World Health Authority" I had to answer "no I was only here to do would ever I could". I realised that my task was to show The Love of God to strengthen these people in their trouble,. I could not cure it but I could show them that God Cared.

The first problem was lack of food all the village supplies had been contaminated so James and I arranged to buy enough rice from another place to give each village family food for three days. We were aware that as soon as the word got out many other people would come as well. So James issued numbered tickets to each family for the rice. We bought as much rice as my credit card would support and some clothes for the women, 5 cwt of rice, and a sari for each lady.

The distribution was planned for that afternoon and the people gathered early, the courtyard was full and the crowd overflowed onto the street outside

It was obvious that there were many more people here than the village community and that we were in for an interesting afternoon.

The distribution started and each lady was to come forward for two jugs of rice to be poured into her apron. This was a slow process and people soon became restless and began to push. Indians do this as part of their culture if ever there is a queue the rule is to get to the front. The ticket system simply ceased to work and it became a free for all. I finished up on the floor twice and my spectacles were in the rice sack three times. However we soldiered on with only one real worry. What would happen when the supply of rice ran out. Towards the evening, as darkness fell, the crowd were satisfied and disappeared. The rice had lasted through out the whole afternoon and when I asked James how many people had been served he could not even guess. I was reminded about loaves and fishes. There may not have been 5000 present and we did not distribute fish, but I knew that God was showing His Power.

I spent three weeks with James and his people and their complaint was that the missionaries always went to the big cities to hold conventions and since, they could not afford to travel, they saw no-one.

I began to see that my purpose would be to spend time with these small churches in places of no apparent importance but to show God's love, care and support for them because they were important to Him.

One evening, as James and I were talking, I asked him how he came to have my address in England. He told me that a lady who supported him also worked for the Birmingham City Mission and had suggested that he get in touch with me because I had helped her some years previously by providing shower cubicles for the Mission. That had been done several years before but the results of our efforts sometimes reappear in ways we could never imagine.

I offered a regular monthly gift to support his work and began to plan my journey back. James took care of the train reservation for me so that was one problem out of the way. I had exhausted all my funds at this time but I had my train ticket and my plane ticket in my pocket and thought that there could not be any more problems.

I left on the night train and James family had packed some sandwiches for the journey. When I opened them they appeared to be a sort of cabbage sandwich. However they went down very well. When the train arrived at Hyderabad I found that I had a 12 hour wait for the Bombay connection. This was not a great problem to start with, I was happy to explore the area around the station and city centre. As midday approached and the temperature started to rise I realised that 12 hours was going to be a longer wait than I had anticipated. In addition I have a very reliable biological clock and it was telling me that I was hungry.

I knew that I had no cash since I had given everything in the village before I left, by going through all my pockets I found a few rupees, about 5p, and started to search for a solution to my problem which would only get worse as the day progressed. I realised that I was not going to die from starvation but still I was hungry.

As I walked along the main streets I saw many dark side alleys but had been warned about them as a European tourist is conspicuous. However one street seemed to be lighter and brighter than the rest and I felt led to go down. It led to a square with three restaurants and one seemed cleaner and brighter so I went in and asked the waiter if it would be possible to have a cup of tea but that I only had this few rupees. He shook his head from side to side as Indians do and went away. A little later he arrived with 2 fried eggs, slices of bread and butter and a pot of tea. At the end of the meal he would accept no payment and as I left the restaurant, I looked back and saw a big bronze plaque over the entrance which read "TRUST IN GOD"

Miracle!!!! - of course.

The rest of my journey was uneventful and when I reached home I told the local paper of the visit and asked if they would feature an appeal to collect clothing and toys for the Indian village children. The local authority gave us permission to take our second ministry bus into town on the next market day. The local New Life Church members supported us and a very large number of local people brought their kids to give toys and clothes for the village children. At the end of the day the bus was so full that I only just had room to get inside and drive it back home. A local firm of shipping agents arranged the transport for us free of charge and a local firm delivered the goods to the dock free as well.

Again we see God at work everywhere and every time.

Chapter 10

Lead Me Heavenly Father

After my return home I was convinced that God had a work for us, in India. We needed to spend time meditating and praying in order to be sure that we set off on the right road. I had seen much of oppression and cruelty in the Indian caste system and the attitude towards women. These areas seemed to be way beyond our capabilities, which is why we needed to be serving according to God's purpose.

There are many possibilities of service in India. Some are large and magnificent others may appear small by comparison. God knows the exact dimension of each task and appoints His servants accordingly. We had learned that we were seed sowers and we began to understand that sowing seed in these apparently impossible situations would be the only way for us to produce fruit. Everyone knows that if you sow seeds plentifully some plants will grow. (Matt 13:8)

I had been told during my conversations with the village pastors, through James as my translator, that they felt isolated and neglected because, as they put it, "all the missionaries go to the big cities and no one ever comes to visit us."

I could do that.

I could see how it would be possible to draw together a group of churches, visiting each one on my annual visits, and maintaining a communication meanwhile by sending a monthly video recording.

I wrote to James to suggest this and asked him to arrange a 10 day conference during my next visit and to invite a suitable group of pastors who could be helpful in this venture.

I was able to go out again several months later and the pastors attended this meeting as arranged. They slept in James's church and each morning we took an Indian breakfast together, spent time in prayer and praise. In the afternoons I had a private time with each pastor so that he could tell me about his particular ministry. Each one told me about his village and the church and local problems. I wanted to glean as much knowledge of their lives as possible on this trip. Our proposed plan was that I would visit each village for 2-3 days once a year in order to spend time with the church and its members, I would send a monthly video teaching and the pastors would meet together to view this and then discuss it.

I had read about the Indian caste system before my first visit and had been led to believe that this was now illegal and was a diminishing problem. I found out from these men that this was most certainly not the case especially in the rural communities. The Caste Hindus still regarded many people as outside the caste system by birth, "out castes". They are excluded from many employments and opportunities.

I also found that when an Indian person becomes a Christian they have to amend their registration form to declare this. They become outcaste, in many cases they lose their employment and any social benefits they may be entitled to.

As an example, on one of my later visits, I travelled, with my translator, by Taxi for 4 hours to reach a pastor's village. When we arrived he was there to meet us and had arranged two bicycles. He insisted that I must go with him to another village by bicycle because there was a man that I must meet. I had not ridden a bike for many years but it is true that the ability never goes away. We travelled about 2 miles down jungle paths and came to a very small hamlet of perhaps 20 huts. I was taken to a hut to meet the man and his wife and two daughters.

His story was that he had been employed by the land owner as the village rat catcher. This gave him a small but regular income. Now that he had become a Christian he had immediately been dismissed from his job.

He told me that his plan was to sell small plastic packets of salt, pepper and herbs from his hut to the village people, and that he wanted me as a Christian business man to pray for him in this venture. I must admit that, in my own strength, I could not see any great prospect for this business. However I prayed with them as a family and promised that I would pray for them and the business from time to time.

On a visit two years later we went again to the same pastor's village and were met with the same 2 bicycles.When we arrived at the small hamlet and met the family I discovered that they now had a small concrete house with a veranda, his wife and daughters were beautifully dressed and he had a beam weighing machine on the veranda. His business had flourished because of his ethical trading and many people were buying rice and spices from him.

This is the beauty of Mustard Seed Working. In the smallest most insignificant places God produces His Miracles. Even when I was, not as faithful as I could have been, God will still work out His plan.

Pastor James was not a young man and he found that it was becoming difficult to travel with me on the village visits. So he introduced me to a man whom I will call Barnabus. He was a younger man and had married one of James' daughters. He was already developing his own ministry and children's home and was keen to serve God in any way that would be put before him. We arranged that our work together would begin on my next visit and Barnabus would visit us in England for a couple of months whilst we made plans for our work together. During that time he visited many local churches with us and addressed the people with his story. He told how he used to go out every day to talk to people and tell them of the love of God. Everyday he and his wife lived on what they had at the time and on one particular morning his wife had said "we have no food or rice at all for today". Never the less Barnabus set off to spread God's word. On his return home at the end of the day he found two abandoned baby girls in the road so he gathered them into his arms and took them home with him, even though he knew that they had no food in the house. When he arrived home he found that someone had left two bags of rice outside their door. Again God does provide for His servants in all contingencies.

Our work together began in January of the following year. January and February are cool months in Southern India and were the most suitable for all the travelling and work that we hoped to do. This became our regular annual visit to the Good News Ministry churches and Children's Homes as we continued to sow seeds in these situations for more than 20 years

Chapter 11

Planted Seeds Begin To Grow

I began a regular correspondence with Barnabus and the group of pastors began to look forward to their monthly meetings together.

At this time Barnabus was living and working entirely by faith, we were able to send our monthly tithe and some support for the pastors travel expenses etc.

This was the whole focus of Mustard Seed working. What we had we gave willingly but it was so GLORIOUSLY small that there was never the slightest danger that people would see it as sufficient to achieve any purpose whatsoever.

Whatever would be achieved would be of God.

Barnabus continued with his own work at the same time. When we first met him, his Children's Home consisted of a lean-to asbestos roof at the back of his house. Over the years we saw that He was blessed with support from other sources and he began to build, IN FAITH a much bigger home and school.

Over the next year or two he sought out other villages and their pastors who were seeking the sort of fellowship and support that we could offer. About this time, Jean suggested that she would like to come with me on a visit so that she could experience these things for herself. So arrangements were made and we set off in early January for another visit. By now our travel arrangements were well organised and it became almost a routine journey. Barnabus met us at Madras airport and took over all our requirements until we arrived at his home.

When we did arrive it was late at night and we were looking forward to a cup of tea, a shower and bed, but we were told that "you cannot sleep here tonight you must get in a taxi and travel for two hours to another place". In this work you learn to trust your fellow workers as well as God.

As the taxi began to enter the village I began to recognise some landmarks and then we saw a house decorated all over with lights and it was James' home. We were delivered into the midst of a Wedding Feast. These events start before the wedding and go for some time after. James daughter Sara was to be married to a young Christian, whom I will call Caleb. I had known Sara since my first visit when she had escorted me around the village and taken great care of me as a guest.

We were privileged to attend a Christian wedding in India and share in the festivities afterwards. I think that Jean did her best to enjoy eating Indian food with her fingers from Banana leaf plates. The young husband was an Indian lawyer and spoke excellent English.

He volunteered to translate for me as we toured the villages for the next few weeks.

We returned to Barnabus home and began our visits to the pastors and congregations. During that time Barnabus told me that he knew of two villages where the children were not attending school because of the distance involved. He wanted to buy two plots of land near each village and build schools where the children could be taught and given a meal every day. Over the next few months we arranged to purchase these plots of land and building began.

A couple of years later Jean came with me again and as we boarded the train we noticed that each carriage was covered in posters announcing a Great Meeting with Missionaries Keith and Mrs Jean Mugglestone to address the people. Complete with Photographs of each of us.

Barnabus had planned all this, and my first thought was that the authorities will not be too pleased about this. However we have come to do what God requires, So Be It.

He had rented the town football pitch and set up a canopy, stage and seating

There were to be three sessions on each of three days, morning evening and a late night meeting. On the first morning about 30 children attended but Barnabus remained confident. "God will send the people ".

Ladies meeting

That night every seat was taken and for the next days programme Barnabus ordered double the number of chairs. They were completely filled and some people were left standing outside. Again for the final day he doubled the number of chairs again and provided extra canopy space. The enclosure was filled again to capacity and people were standing outside the area to listen

Men's Meeting

The meeting finished at about midnight with an alter call and then a prayer line began to form. This is a normal occurrence in these events and the temptation is to pronounce a standard prayer and move on to the next person.

I had decided from the very beginning that I would never do this. Each person was to be listened to and understood and then that prayer was to be SPECIFIC unto that persons needs.

We arrived back at Barnabus home at about 3.30 in the morning and the Police arrived shortly after. Barnabus told us to stay in our room and not to come out in any circumstances. Later he came to tell us that there had been a Hindu complaint about our big noisy meeting, he had told the Police that we had already left so they went away satisfied, we hoped! This was our first real taste of the discrimination and hatred that militant Christians face in India. Our pastors were used to it and they endured and remained faithful

Persecution toughens Christians, Comfort softens them.

Chapter 12

The plants begin to mature and bear fruit

Shortly after our return to England we received a letter from Caleb telling us that since his wedding and his work translating for me in the village visits,

a "Sea Change" had come over his life and he now wanted to devote himself to God's work. He asked if it would be possible for him to do this along with Barnabus and myself.

Barnabus' work was growing and it was demanding more and more of his time, He told me that he had encouraged Caleb to write to me.

Caleb and I had worked well together during the ministry visits. It is essential to have a good relationship with your translator, if the thrust of the message is not to be diluted by someone who is not in harmony with you.

We agreed together that we would arrange for Caleb to begin his work with us on my next visit.

The time for that visit seemed to come around very quickly and I was soon on board a plane once more bound for India. I was to stay with Barnabus and enjoy meeting his family and the children in the home. By now the ground floor of the new children's home was complete and Barnabus had negotiated an arrangement with the government. They would fund the construction of a second storey if it would be made available for use as a flood refuge for the local villagers when necessary.

I was taken to Caleb's town and he took me to see their new home. I had to climb a ladder up to a small door which gave access to a bare roof space or loft. There was no natural lighting or ventilation and it was unbearably hot. I told him that he must move his wife and himself out of there immediately and find something much more suitable and we would worry about the cost later. It did not take them very long as there is a good supply of property to rent and to Europeans the rents appear to be incredibly low. They soon settled into a nice little 4 roomed house on a quiet street.

They had chosen to live in the loft because that was all that they could afford. Now that he had to be the sole provider for both of them he discovered that an outcaste lawyer, no matter how well qualified will only be allowed to take cases from the poor people who cannot afford to pay anyway. Again this is the same unseen influence that attempts to "steal and kill and destroy" Christians everywhere. John 10:10.

The battle is a spiritual one only to be won by faith and endurance.

We planned for Caleb to visit us in England for a couple of months in the summer, after he and Sara had settled into their new home, so that we could plan and organise our work together. We were able to introduce him to many local churches and he became more assured in his delivery and his second language, English. It was delightful to see how this young man yielded to the leading of the Holy Spirit. He had experienced the treatment the world had offered to him on many occasions throughout his youth and now he only wanted God and His fellowship and guidance.

He was still a young man but I looked forward to seeing him Grow, Develop and Bear fruit.

Barnabus' larger children's home was now up and running, as well as the 2 schools in the isolated villages. The teachers who were responsible for those schools were two of Barnabus' first orphans who had grown up, trained as teachers and returned to work with Him in the schools.

The completed School in Oeration

It is a constant source of delight to me to see how God produces just the right people at just the exact time for every situation. A good magician may produce a rabbit out of a hat, God does so much more!!!.

Trials, temptations and victories.

During my next visit the Indian television news announced that war had broken out in Iraq and that all flights across the Middle Eastern routes had been suspended for an unknown period.

My visit still had three more weeks to go and it was possible that I may be stranded here for an unknown period. I could allow this problem to distract us from our work or we could carry on, remembering how God had undertaken for everything up till now.

We redoubled our efforts for the remainder of the time and then I went to Madras hoping to be able to catch my flight. Everything appeared to be normal and I boarded the plane in due course. The Captain announced that the route would be changed to avoid the troubled airspace but he said "do not worry we will get you there"

Once more, the Enemy puts fear and difficulties in front of us, but if we continue to move in faith God is invariably greater.

Here is yet another illustration of God's Grace and power. On one occasion when Jean was with me, a pastor told us that one of his women church members wanted to take baptism but that she was afraid of the reaction of her Hindu husband if she did this. Hindu women are not allowed to speak to an unknown man, so I was unable to do anything, however Jean offered to meet with this lady and pray for her. The lady continued in her commitment to be baptised. When she returned home she found that her husband had thrown out all the Hindu idols and pictures from the house and he announced that he wanted to become a Christian together with his wife.

Chapter 13

Good seed into good ground brings forth much fruit

The people always did their best to care for us whenever we visited but their resources were very limited. For us it was a privilege to be welcomed into their homes and share life with them for a few days. I remember how on one visit to a jungle village a dear old lady came to greet me by offering an egg and a banana as her gift. As she proffered these gifts she knelt and kissed my feet. They have so little to give and yet they offer something beyond measure. These memories bring me to my knees in humble gratitude for the privilege of being allowed to serve in this work.

On Jean's last visit we were sitting on a bench in a square in Madras and noticed a young English woman and her young daughter sitting opposite to us. They were obviously both in severe distress and after a while I approached them to see if we could help. The story was that their hotel room had been robbed and all their money taken. The hotel had thrown them out and retained their luggage until they could pay. The banks were closed and they had nothing for food or accommodation. We gave them sufficient cash to take care of their present needs. She told me that she could transfer cash when the bank reopened next day. They expressed their gratitude and went on their way. We never heard from them again but once more SEED had been sown.

The return journey had been hot and difficult we had decided to fly back using India's internal airline hoping that it would be more comfortable than the long train journey. There was a flight change in Hyderabad but the ongoing flight would be delayed for an unspecified time. The transit area was a tin shed and the heat was going to be unbearable throughout the afternoon. I did not know what we could do about this but I knew a God who did. It was only a short prayer and a big grey American limousine whispered up and parked. A young man in a suit came up to us and asked if we would like a hotel room. I cautiously enquired about the cost and he told me that if we would take a meal in their restaurant they would take care of our luggage, provide a room and shower for the afternoon FREE of charge. The hotel was magnificent, the food delicious and God's care was "immeasurably more than all we ask or imagine" Eph. 3:20.

When I returned home from the early visits I found that it took a week or so to recover from the Indian tummy upsets etc. Now however after each visit it was taking up to six months to get back to normal. It was obviously time to ease off.

I now began to realise that the years were beginning to catch up on me after more than twenty years of visits, living in rural village conditions with variable water and other supplies often from unknown sources.

I managed one or two more visits over the next few years and saw that the churches, pastors and children's homes were now self sufficient and maturing. It is just like a family which grows up and needs to leave the parents nest. As long as "they straighten up and fly right" then All is Well.

The pastors that had English were able to correspond with us to keep us up to date with the work.

Caleb visited us once more on one of his English visits to the churches we had introduced him to.

In 2008 Barnabus sent a card announcing that he had completed his M.Theology degree and was now appointed Bishop over his substantial group of churches. The Orphan's home was now fully complete and the card showed large groups of the children, possibly well over one hundred.

In 2014 In England Neal and Philip attended a leaders meeting of the group of churches that they work with. It is the form at these meetings, for visiting leaders to introduce themselves.

A dark man introduced himself as Caleb from Southern India where he was superintendent of The Good News Ministry which had been founded by Keith Mugglestone nearly 40 years ago.

"A mustard seed is the smallest of all your seeds yet when it grows it becomes a tree and the birds of the air come and perch in its branches". Matt 13:31.32.

Barnabus Orphans Home

Chapter 14

My People will live in
Peaceful Dwelling-places
In secure homes,
in undisturbed places of rest.
Isaiah.32:18

We found that "it was good" to spend time for longer periods in rural Lincolnshire instead of always being up and doing. I was under instructions from the family to take it steady now and enjoy your retirement.

Our home was called Stillwater Cottage because He had led us to a place "beside the Still Waters" We were able to worship in the local churches that we had grown to love so well and we could also enjoy times out on the boat.

During one winter, Neal and I did a Yacht Masters Course. It was good to spend some father and son time together over a common project. During the following summer we began to explore the coast line as well as river work.

We now had the ability to venture further with the boat and a small seed started to germinate in my soul... THE URGE to "do something new" appeared again.

I had no idea what form this might take but that was not a problem, anything God put in front of us would be wonderful.

Occasionally we used to purchase a magazine in which people could buy and sell things. One of its sections was devoted to land and property and I saw an advert for a complete farm in Spain for £4000. Once again I had no knowledge of Spain and had never been tempted to visit. I suppose I should realise that if we ask God to do Something New then we should not be surprised if it is just that. Completely and unexpectedly New.

In an attempt to "put out a fleece" I asked God to arrange an immediate flight and a visit which would reveal without any doubt that this was indeed His Purpose. We had an idea of what the ideal situation would look like and out of all the sites that the agent showed us, one leapt out as being absolutely right.

I told the agent that it was suitable but that I also needed to have my boat out here as well. We visited a local marina and they had one mooring suitable for a boat of our size and so we made arrangements for the land and mooring there and then we took "the Fleece" back in, we did not need a second test, and proceeded to plan the voyage from England to Spain.

The boat would need to be up graded for the long voyage and we planned to be in Spain by September so we would leave England in July.

In the week before we were due to leave Jean had a fall in the market square and injured her wrist. She chose to strap it up with an elastic bandage and carry on with our plan regardless. Neal and one of his friends came with us as crew and we set off down the river and out across the North Sea to Belgium. Neal's friend had a theory that ginger biscuits were a good protection against sea sickness. As we left the calm river and met the sea swell he began munching ginger biscuits. He soon found out that they did not quite fulfil their promise. It became obvious that he would not manage the crossing especially if the weather turned rough. So we had to put into Yarmouth harbour so that he could phone his girl friend to come and rescue him.

The next morning we were ready to leave again and I was standing on the harbour wall when I stepped backward and fell about 8 ft onto the road. I landed on my arm which became extremely painful and swollen. We continued the voyage with two good arms between Jean and I together. Jean had a good left arm and I had my right one we were a little like "Jack Spratt and his wife".

As we got out into the open sea we felt the full force of the head wind and the boat began to work its way ahead. Punching into each wave she buried her bow into them one by one, threw off the spray over the cabin roof and then rose up and over ready for the next.

Neal sat at the helm, vomiting through the side window from time to time and all I had to do was just keep those two diesels running. Trying to plot a course on a chart was totally impossible it was all we could do to stay on our feet. I decided to plot a direct course to steer.

I reckoned that in the 12 hour crossing we would meet both tides which would cancel out most of the drift. My real consolation was that Europe has a good long coastline. If we hit Sweden we would turn right and work our way down and on the other hand if we made landfall in Portugal we could turn left and work our way back.

The night passed slowly but eventually dawn broke and we saw seagulls, a sure sign that land is near. As the day brightened we could see the coast line ahead and there smack on the bow was a harbour wall with big white letters

Zeebrugge

Praise The Lord

We entered the harbour tied up and put the kettle on.

Neal booked a return passage on the next ferry whilst we completed the formalities with the customs and harbour master. We stayed over night for a rest before beginning the next stage, canal navigation all across France to the Mediterranean coast.

We cast off early the next morning and went through a large lock out of the harbour into a canal network. The canals in Belgium and France run mainly through the industrial areas or open countryside. They are often lined on both banks by trees the water reflects the green light percolating down through the leaves and the atmosphere is green and peaceful with many quiet stretches with little traffic if any. There are tourist centres with hire boats which are allowed to run with no licence and very little training. They can be easily recognised by the multitude of fenders that are fitted to protect the poor boat from the many bumps and ricochets that they have to endure. Usually they tend to stay fairly close to their base and so we were soon past them.

French Canal

We tied up every Saturday so that we could keep Sundays special for rest and worship. On one such weekend we were in the Champagne region and had tied up near a wide expanse of open land in a small town. In the afternoon a man approached us and began to talk to us in French. We only have school French but we understood that he wanted to meet with us. We invited him on board and made an English cup of tea to share with him. The gist of the conversation was that they were Catholics and went to the local church. We did our best mime of understanding and the conversation seemed to go extremely well. When he had enjoyed his tea he left us and went across the land to a row of houses. About half an hour later he returned with a bunch of flowers for Madam and told us that his wife wanted to meet us, so would we come to their home in the evening at Sept hours and his house number was Neuf .... something. When it was time we set off feeling a little foolish in case we knocked on the wrong

Neuf....... house. However all went well and we were invited in and served Champagne (of course) and biscuits. They both talked to us enthusiastically and we did our best to keep up, more or less. As the evening drew to a close we thanked them and prepared to leave. The man then asked us to come again on Monday morning before we left so that we could meet his son. We did meet the son, had a short chat and then set off on our journey.

We had no idea of their reason for doing this unless it was simply that The Lord brought us together to be a pleasant blessing to each other.

Most French canal locks are automatic so that the chore of winding paddles and gates by hand is removed. On our journey we also passed through two tunnels which had been cut through a range of hills when the canal was constructed one was nearly 2 miles long and the other more than that. They are unlit and it requires great attention to thread a wide boat between the brick walls without doing too much damage

We travelled for the whole week gradually covering the route and then on Saturday afternoon we tied up ready for our weekend. Another boat came onto the same mooring later, It's name was MUSTARD SEED and they were a Canadian couple so of course we had a good weekend together. They were Christians and their reason for making this journey together was that the husband had terminal cancer and this would be his last adventure here on earth. They had sailed their small sailing boat across the Atlantic in three weeks and were now cruising as much of Europe as they could in the time left to them. Their faith was rock solid and we were blessed to spend time with them.

Amazing Grace on Canal

We found shopping in France to be interesting some times due to language problems. The Microwave cooker on our boat had died and we needed another one. We visited a large store which sold Domestic electrical goods and I had carefully looked up the right word for microwave, it was micro- onde. I caught the attention of a sales person and explained that I wanted to buy a micro- onde The blank look on his face was one of absolute non comprehension. After several attempts I went into the mime. By now we had attracted other staff and a small group of helpful shoppers. I explained that you take a poulet and ouvre la porte of the cabinette, insert said poulet and switch on. Wizzy wizzy wizzy and then ping. Suddenly comprehension dawned and he said "Oh Micro-ondes we don't sell them here".

Later on we came across the King David boat and the couple that had called on us in Boston. We spent some time with them catching up on their story. They were enjoying their canal life style and keeping faithful with video cassettes and Christian books. We were able to keep in touch and visit them occasionally when later we used to drive through France on our visits to our family.

We crossed France by canal in about four weeks and reached Marseille ready for the run down the French and Spanish coast to our new mooring.

Chapter 15

Your Land Will Be Called Beulah. Isa 62;3-4.

As we travelled down the French and Spanish coast we found that there are marinas with visitor's berths in most coastal towns. So the voyage was fairly simple we moored safely every night with all services available and cruised a comfortable distance each day.

Coastal navigation in Spain is especially simple, you can mange without the need to calculate or read a chart, although such foresight is always advisable. It is quite possible to look over the side of the boat and read the name of the town we are passing from the name on the plastic shopping bags which are floating all around. This is a sad reflection on our ecological housekeeping, but at least it works as a navigation aid.

We arrived at the Club Nautic and identified our berth which was all prepared and ready, so we tied up and considered the voyage well and truly completed. The Club Staff were the first to call on us their only concern was that we should be comfortable and happy. We soon discovered the Club Nautic membership had developed a family relationship together and we drawn into this.

We planned to live aboard the boat as we sorted out the land and began to build Beulah. As we pondered over the choice of a name for our new home we were led to Isaiah 62:3-4.

"You will be a crown of splendour in the Lord's hand,

a royal diadem in the hand of your God.

No longer will they call you deserted,

But you will be called Hephzibah,

And your land Beulah;

For the Lord will take delight in you,

And your land will be married."

We have found over the ensuing years that this has come to pass in many ways. What was an abandoned land stripped bare and sold as worthless has been loved and husbanded, it now blooms, and it seems to be a delight to all who visit here. We have learned that whatever God provides for any of His Loving Children is always "a pearl beyond price".

We obtained planning permission to build a garage/workshop for my small collection of classic cars which I hoped to bring out to Spain. We employed local labour and the work began.

Building Foundations

The work began to progress fairly smoothly, although in the normal Spanish leisurely fashion, and we began to search more widely for Christian fellowship and worship. There are Catholic churches even in the small towns, but this is Catalonia and they are very committed to preserving their Catalan dialect. A Catholic liturgy in the Catalan dialect was going to be very strange for us at this time so we toured for many miles North and South looking in nearly every town for a church which practised the free and spirit filled worship that we related to. It seemed as though we could not find one wherever we looked.

We had established a routine of talking to the family every Sunday evening by phone. I mentioned to Neal that we were having this difficulty and he told me that in that morning's service in their church a couple of missionaries from Spain had been addressing the congregation and announced that an American evangelist from the AOG church was on his way to start a new church in Tarragona, a city a comfortable distance from where we lived. Again God provides and we find our trust in His Miraculous providence confirmed and reinforced on an almost daily basis.

We arranged to meet this missionary to discuss any future opportunity that might be possible it was obvious from the first moment that this would be a golden opportunity for us both to work together and build whatever The Lord had planned. I shall call this pastor "Luke".

He had rented a shop premises in the ground floor of a block of flats in an urban housing development and his church was just beginning to come together. We attended on Sundays to support them and during the week we began to see how our work in Spain would be different from anything we had done before. Luke found that his church drew Spanish people seeking a fuller relationship with God but there was considerable resistance from the traditional community who saw no need for any departure from the established tradition. Our opportunity was to be towards the Expatriate English who felt that their life style was already established.

We needed God to provide openings into these lives so that a Seed of Witness could be sown. I realised that this would be to one person or one family at a time. So I was asking Father to send me "just one more "opportunity to witness (with the proviso that when that was complete I would probably ask again "just one more please").

The first opportunity was soon provided on a Sunday morning. We were sitting on the rear deck of the boat enjoying Spanish sunshine and our Spanish style breakfast of Cornflakes, Fresh Strawberries and Spanish champagne, (never mind what the French say about it, we love it.)

A Spanish car pulled up on the quayside and the driver brought his passenger towards us. He explained that this man was English but he couldn't understand him so he had brought him to us. We invited this man onboard, he was very confused and distressed so we offered him breakfast and listened to his story. He had responded to an advert for Bar/restaurants for sale in Spain. The agents met him at the airport and he had given them a deposit in cash. They then showed him 20 such properties in 2 hours, which left him totally confused, they asked him which one he wanted to buy? When he asked for time to consider the matter they walked away and left him with no Spanish money, and a flat that they had rented for one night. It was Saturday and the Banks would not open until Monday.

We withdrew some cash from a bank machine for which he gave us English Pounds, then we needed to find a supermarket which was open so that he could buy some supplies. We also arranged for the flat to be available until he was ready to catch his flight. That solved his immediate problems but he was still feeling very lost and alone. So we brought him back to the boat and spent the rest of the day with him. Naturally in due time the conversation turned to matters Spiritual he sincerely believed that "this stuff" no longer existed and the fact anyone still considered this to be important was new to him. Eventually he was ready to return to his flat and then catch his flight back to England. I gave him a spiritual book and my son's phone no. so that he could keep in touch with us if he wished. Neal told me that they had some quite long conversations with him on two occasions.

Luke's church continued to grow the Spanish people who attended wanted a fuller relationship with God and some were already Spirit filled. Luke had excellent American Spanish and I was able to preach from time to time and he would translate for me.

The workshop building was now complete and I was ready to bring my classic cars out from England. A neighbour warned me that isolated properties were often burgled. I felt that we should have a suitably large guard dog on the land to deter these bad people. A German shepherd breed seemed to be ideal but thoroughbred dogs are very expensive in Spain and we were working to a fairly tight budget as usual. So again we leave these problems in God's hands. One afternoon I was kneeling down working on a car and l felt a big wet lick on the back of my neck. When I turned round there was a fully grown Alsatian dog looking at me. She had a frayed piece of rope around her neck so she had probably been abandoned or escaped; We made no attempt to contain her for some weeks so that if she chose to return she could.. She never did and became the guard dog that we had asked for

Miracle. ....Or Course.

Luke meanwhile needed to return home to visit his father who was terminally ill. His return flight had a 2 day stopover in England so I suggested that he visit Neal and family at Still Water cottage for the 2 days. He was pleased to do this and they got on well together. Americans have a fascination with red English double-decker buses and when he heard about our bus ministry in the past he wanted to examine the possibility of such work. There is always a man in Lincolnshire who specialises in any subject you may mention. There was such a man locally who had several red London Buses. Neal took Luke to meet him and Luke ordered 2 immediately. We could imagine who would be asked to arrange for these to come to Spain!

It all "came to pass", as it would, I drove one to our place and Neal later drove the other with his young family on board to Madrid. Both trips were exciting adventures.

When Luke tried to register these buses for use in Spain the red tape was unbelievable. They were Right Hand drive of course and they didn't like that. To drive a bus in Spain the driver must complete a Spanish course taking about 2 years and the minimum insurance available would be about £6,000 a year. This blew the concept straight out of the window but I was able to keep our bus registered as an English vehicle and drive it on my licence and insurance. We managed to do this for just over a year. By which time Luke's 3 year contract was coming to a close. Another Pastor was sent but he had no Spanish so the church became a community church with Spanish congregation and leadership. Eventually we lost contact with them.

Red Bus

By this time we had built most of the house at Beulah and were spending more time here than on the boat. One Saturday afternoon we were sitting on the patio enjoying the sunshine when a stranger arrived. He came in and we could see that he had something on his mind, so we waited and kept the conversation light until it came blurting out. He said" I have been told that if anybody comes here they will get "Godded." I want to be "Godded". He worshipped with us and learned a lot in the next two years but has not yet been able to detach himself from his previous life style.

Beulah Patio

We still visited the boat weekly to check on things and spend some time onboard. One day when we visited we were pleased to see another boat flying the English Red Ensign. It meant that we would be able to meet and spend time with other English boat people.

We saw a young couple pushing a baby in a buggy along the quayside so I went up to meet them the man said "you probably won't want to talk to us because we've been impounded". I didn't really know what impounded entailed but it sounded like trouble to me. So I asked for the story, and they had moored out in the bay and a strong wind had caused their anchor to drag, they had collided with the mussel farm in the bay and done some damage. The mussel farmer had made a charge and the authorities had brought their boat into the harbour and chained it up until the matter was resolved.

The farmer was making a very inflated claim and the harbour charges were £40 a day. The young man had minimal Spanish, his girl friend and her child had gone back home with her father. So he felt that his cup of bitterness was full if not overflowing. I took all his damaged handrails and fittings to the workshop and soon had things straightened welded and fitted. At least now his boat looked better. We then spent time with him and found that he was receptive to hear God's word. We lead him to the Lord and then we had to return to England for a 3 week visit.

When we returned we asked him how things had progressed. He told us that every day he felt that he should go to a church to pray and that he had done this. The court had moved the hearing forward as a matter of urgency and the lifeboat crew that had recovered his boat and towed it in to the harbour testified that the damage to the mussel farm was only slight a few timber posts and some rope. The judge resolved the case saying that the boat should be released as soon as the young man had paid for the timber posts and ropes.

Having heard how long Spanish court cases can take,

Once again

I ask - A Miracle.....YES.

Chapter 16

Complete The Race
And Finish The Task
Acts. 20:24

This brings our story up to date, and we are able to see where we are at this present moment but there is still more to do.

Our family business has survived some ups and downs but is still functioning after more than 50 years with the third generation of the family now actively involved.

Our Christian service has been varied and always stimulating and our relationship with Father deeply rewarding and delightful.

In both these areas we now understand that it is time to hand over the baton.

In the business Neal is gradually handing over management to Grandson Joshua and he is showing increasing maturity and wisdom. We look forward with confidence to seeing further growth and fruitfulness in it

In our joint Christian walk,

Neal has now become Senior Pastor of a Boston Church.

Davina continues to play the piano (as she did when we first met her) and leads the music and worship team.

Granddaughter Hannah serves in the children's work in the church and is now The CAP (Christians Against Poverty) representative for the Boston Area.

Joshua plays the drums for worship and also serves with the sound desk and everything else that people ask for.

"Becky" (Youngest granddaughter, Rebecca.) Plays guitar for worship services and helps in the children's group.

In the other arm of the family;

Son in law Philip is involved as a house group leader and in other roles in their local Church

Daughter Wendy is still working as Head Teacher of a private School with a strong Christian ethos and also serves in their local church.

Granddaughter Emma is now married to Luke and they both teach but in different schools. They are leaders of a recent offspring church in their local area.

Emma is expecting to give us our first Great Grand child soon.

Grandson Andrew has graduated from Cambridge as an electrical engineer and is working locally with the design and testing of equipment for water supply installations. He continues to shine as an outstanding example of a young Christian man.

Jean and I remain convinced after nearly 60 years together that God engineered our meeting and He has developed our bond ever more strongly over the years.

We still see a road ahead and are eager to walk it. Our goal is that wonderful greeting "well done, good and faithful servant"

Chapter 17

Conclusion

WHAT HAVE WE LEARNED SO FAR

Many people tell me. "I do not have the faith to do things like that".

We must remember that Jesus had this same discussion with His disciples when they were unable to heal a sick boy. Matt.17:14-20.

Jesus told us, "ask and you will receive" meaning that whatever we ask for, as believers under His guidance, he will provide but does He not further encourage us in this by saying, I can make available to you all of Eph.3:20. "immeasurably more than all we can ask for or imagine, according to his power that is at work in us".

More than we can imagine? Is it our lack or imagination or hope or faith that limits us or DARE we REALLY believe that, "Nothing is impossible to God".

Faith does not come in different sizes it starts small (as a mustard seed) and grows. That growth depends on the development of our relationship with The Father, Son and Holy Spirit

The more we grow in that relationship the more we are able to move and work in faith.

I firmly believe that this growth depends more on the relationship than it does upon knowledge.

Unfortunately knowledge is acquired more comfortably than we can develop a deeper relationship

We can acquire knowledge by reading, studying and attending conferences and such. All of which provide a strong foundation for THE RELATIONSHIP to grow upon.

The Relationship is personal and intimate. It is individual and unique to each of us. One of the more Glorious gifts that God offers to us.

The closer and deeper our relationship grows the more we find that He is able to work through us. Zec.4:6 "not by might nor by power but by my Spirit."

Our relationship develops in this way.

FIRST We meet and receive The Father who offers his grace and forgiveness

Then we meet and receive His Son who purchased our salvation and freedom.

Then we meet and receive The Holy Spirit from whom we receive POWER.

Acts.1;8 "You will receive power when the Holy Spirit comes upon you".

There are three persons in the Godhead. Does it not seem logical that we should need all three to "do the work that God requires." John.6:28

If it is in the book just do it!

Acknowledgments

Bible quotations are from the New International Version (NIV)

Copyright 1978 by New York International Bible Society

The song." Do something New Lord" By Chris Bowater

Copyright 1986 Sovereign Lifestyle Music